EMOTIONAL INTELLIGENCE

EMOTIONAL INTELLIGENCE

Enhancing Your EQ for Success

AVERY NIGHTINGALE

QuillQuest Publishers

CONTENTS

1 Introduction 1
2 Developing Self-Awareness 6
3 Building Empathy and Social Skills 11
4 Applying Emotional Intelligence in Various Areas 16

Copyright © 2024 by Avery Nightingale

All rights reserved. No part of this book may be reproduced in any manner whatsoever without written permission except in the case of brief quotations embodied in critical articles and reviews.

First Printing, 2024

CHAPTER 1

Introduction

These two results lead to a life that is happier than you ever dreamed it could be. Let me underline and make myself absolutely clear: for many many years, I carried out research, studying people's emotional intelligence; over and over again, the results revealed that these so-called emotionally-intelligent people were always more successful and more satisfied at their work and in their private lives and most of all, they were healthier. When people understand that it's their thoughts about their feelings that make them what they are, that their illogical conclusions affect how they feel, when they understand where and how their feelings come from, look at their emotions (in order to understand them) are able to manage them (using their logic), you can see that all the other aspects of their life tend to function more correctly too and this is why they are healthier. This last aspect has a strong scientific basis since all psychologists know that living in a context where emotions are openly referred to and accepted leads to a better degree of physical and psychological health. So, as you read this book, you will understand why emotions are important, much more important than what we all believe; it's not true that reason and sentiments are two separate entities; you'll have understood that science tells us that reason cannot manage without our emotions and also that education is a mark of our emotional competences.

In this self-reflective guide, we will look at your emotional intelligence or your EQ, giving you new insight into how emotions don't only matter, they are the keys to success in life, the most important factor that differentiates people and accounts for their success or failure in relationships and also, at work. We will look at what emotional intelligence is, at where emotions come from and, after we know where they come from, you will understand how they develop; you can then take your allotted control, your decision-making capability to your emotions which will prevent you from sabotaging your life's chances and choices. We will also look at how emotions that are intelligently managed help you to have healthier, agreeable, nearer and more continuous friendships and family relationships and are the basis of a successful career.

1.1. What is Emotional Intelligence?

A simpler version of the tension involved is that feeling is on the side of the heart, head is on, well, the side of the head. Heart versus head: we seem primed to oppose the two. Now it's emotional intelligence versus traditional intelligence. Franklin Roosevelt intentionally played to the contrast by saying that a person needed to be 'a Bible student, a student of history... -and a keen student of human nature' to be successful. Such people would need to be as good at evaluating and guiding their own and others' emotions as they were at analyzing other data. We know that success requires good skills in any such key area. But assessing and developing emotional intelligence turned out to be very difficult. It's clear that different emotional states can combine to create complex emotions. Maybe the expressions associated with these different states could be quite different, but Richards and his team asked many volunteers to keep diaries and note down the physical sensations associated with twelve everyday emotions.

The concept of emotional intelligence (or EQ) dates back at least to the mid-1920s, when Edward Thorndike used the phrase while referring to a person's range of skills - such as the ability to perceive and manage one's emotions, and the ability to be sympathetic towards others. But the idea of emotional intelligence enjoyed a renaissance when Daniel

Goleman's book, Emotional Intelligence, brought it to widespread attention in 1995. If your eyes didn't precisely widen in amazement then, they might now: the concept of EQ has proved popular and enduring. That's partly because it aims to be a simple, practical guide to understanding and applying the essential ingredient of success. (Goleman did it again in his follow-up book, Social Intelligence: The New Science of Human Relationships.)

1.2. Importance of Emotional Intelligence

Emotional intelligence has become a hot topic nowadays. It is about understanding emotions and their causes. It is being aware of your feelings and the feelings of others. It is learning how to communicate with whatever we come across in life. A person should start understanding the need for becoming emotionally intelligent. The more emotionally intelligent a person becomes, the more successful they will be in their professional life, as well as their personal life. It can help predict success in life. When you are able to control your feelings and emotions, you can prevent unwanted feelings from being important. You can assess people's behavior and respond to their emotions. It is an ability to control and handle your emotions. Emotional intelligence is about understanding your emotions as well as understanding other people. It is important to try to comprehend and develop your communication skills. With enhanced skills in this area, you will speak more clearly, and people will clearly understand what you are saying. You will also get across the point that you are driving to pass.

Emotions are a very powerful force, and they have the potential to control our lives. Just about everything we do is based upon our feelings and emotions. We have created the success and failures that we are living with. In today's world, maintaining focus and drive is very important if you want to achieve success. A person can possess a high IQ but can be of very little use if they lack the ability to control their feelings and emotions. Whether working in your professional life or personal life, you need to be aware of your feelings and the feelings of others. One of the reasons some people struggle is that they do not know how to interact with other individuals. When you understand yourself and have full control over your feelings, you will find that you can better understand how to interact with other individuals and how to control your relationships.

1.3. Benefits of Enhancing Your EQ

Developing emotional intelligence empowers you with the skills of self-awareness, self-confidence, motivation, self-control, empathy, and effective communication - all of which are necessary to attain personal and business success. It increases your feelings of self-worth, confidence, and charisma. You will come across to others as "together", or as a person who is understanding, approachable, and caring. It promotes your enthusiasm, inspiration, and intrinsic motivation. You are more likely to approach new challenges, have a positive attitude, and be a catalyst for goal setting and success in others. It fosters your ability to perceive, understand, express, and manage your feelings. In times of adversity, you remain flexible and easygoing. Additionally, you are capable of seeing things from different perspectives. You make sound, confident decisions, which positively influence consumer behaviors and purchasing decisions in business settings. These effective business decisions could entail inventory purchases, supply chain distribution, employee financial benefits, etc. It promotes a cooperative atmosphere, encouraging others to understand, clarify, and solve problems. You will make informed business decisions, protect customer relationships, and engage in non-confrontational discussions without alienating partners in the bargaining process.

The aim of emotional intelligence is to educate people to become more emotionally skilled, to become more aware of others' feelings and in turn to become more successful in their social relationships at home and at work. Damasio reminds us that: '...each one of us would lead a private emotional life, just for personal use and understanding, if there were no social interactions' (Damasio, 1994, p 191). You know that EQ's not just about having a nice personality. More and more studies prove that EQ is as important, if not more important, than IQ when it comes to being successful in almost all facets of life. Here are some of the amazing benefits of enhancing your EQ.

CHAPTER 2

Developing Self-Awareness

Emotions are often uniquely personal but in a very real way affect everyone around us. In fact, emotions exert a sort of magnetic power in most groups. Emotions are the force that shapes and controls a group's dynamics. Based on a wealth of data and several quantitative measures, including perceived group performance, emotions predict a majority of the performance variance in group members. In addition to influencing your members' verbal behaviors, from a person's emotional expression flows such nonverbal behavior as body movements, gestures, and facial expressions. Such behavior can reinforce or contradict the words spoken, providing cues to the alignment of the speaker's attitudes and intentions and to the interactive dynamics between small groups or even between customers.

Every successful leader knows that self-awareness is a critical factor in optimizing personal growth. To become self-aware, then, a leader must be aggressively committed to empowering those around them to help them see themselves as they truly are. The power of this concept is that once leaders get a detailed and accurate account of their particular style and situational impact, they can then realistically choose to change. It is a pivotal process in a leader's total self-management cycle. Understanding our MBTI type is the first key in building self-awareness. Documenting our sourcing matrix is next. After checking for our sources of strengths and weaknesses, our self-management team members should complete and process another questionnaire.

2.1. Recognizing and Managing Emotions

One approach to emotional management is to increase self-awareness of when and how certain emotions arise. For instance, within the context of taking charge of our feelings, each time we sense sadness, we could take a short moment to examine how we feel and to fully understand that we are, indeed, experiencing sadness. Having realized that we are feeling a certain emotion, we are more prepared to manage it. Another approach to emotional management is to actually become good at experiencing discomfort. Basically, we should stop running from our negative emotions. Some people spontaneously choose this second approach; they have learned that a good way to handle the expression of emotion is to experience them and to also clearly express them whenever they need to. With this in mind, these individuals exhibit calmness over the longer run. They must be realists and exhibit an almost reverent approach when it comes to offering solutions. These simple strategies, which to the onlooker might even seem exaggerated, are often more effective. Several research studies in the field of cognitive psychology indicate that cognitive therapy is effective at controlling and changing dysfunctional behavior.

To begin with, managing our emotions looks at using techniques to stop or reduce emotional reactions. This, in turn, stops inappropriate actions and the possibility of deepening the damage often associated with strong emotional outbursts. Strategies focusing on how to stop an emotional reaction are also skills in optimizing emotions, in terms of creation, utilization, and energy flow. We can manage our emotions in a number of different ways. The emotional components we can manage are tension, sadness, and anger. We should keep in mind that these components do not affect us all at the same time or with the same intensity. Furthermore, our current mood heavily influences how we interpret and handle our emotions. As a quick example, if we are in a good mood, we often manage our emotions with more humor.

2.2. Understanding Personal Triggers

In situations that could not be controlled by the individual, just like the trauma experienced by the author, these mental models become negative and they cloud our true judgment resulting in unwarranted thoughts and actions. These mental models are psychological relationships that are formed through concepts wired in the brain. They form the basis of emotional rationality that may be reliable in many instances. The author illustrates that these negative mental models can be formed when adult propositions are made by a five-year-old, which is not the case in the aforementioned situation but these situations have firsthand judgmental problems due to the different perspectives formed over the years of being socialized.

People tend to have different personal triggers. These triggers or circumstances affect our thought patterns and, if misunderstood, are capable of determining our overall judgment. As a result, we need to be mindful of all these elements so as to develop a self-understanding that will invariably enable us to create a better personal attitude. Now that we are acquainted with triggers, it is important to note that these triggers emerge as a result of different perspectives we have in certain situations. It is also possible to view these perspectives or attitudes as mental models formed by years of learning and socialization that employ a certain amount of emotion to create thought trends.

2.3. Cultivating Emotional Resilience

To me, the greatest message was that the cultivation and practice of martial arts have not only broadened the heroes' studied applications of combat excellence but also shaped their hearts and minds to resolve challenges and crises with the focused martial spirit and emotional resilience. These short phraseology can be summarized as EI-Enhancing and Emotional Resilience because emotions are the integral influences on us. Emotional resilience is not the absence of emotions nor stoicism but the freedom to transcend emotions and the expressions of the assortment of feelings via constructive and useful measures despite extenuating circumstances. Leadership begins from the inside-out and "authentically talented" leaders discern their own fearlessness, passion, resolution, wisdom, compassion, loyalty, and respect in the interdimension of their spirit. When they unearth their deepest sincerity to reach inwards and touch their true intuitive self, they will set foot on a journey that climbs to the next growth phase of their leadership life. With their rising self-awareness, their conscious leadership choices transform potent leaders into "resilient navigators" from conflict or from the crossroads of their life.

In mid-2011, two new movies about the lives of martial art exponents were released: Ip Man II and The Legend is Born. I took my family members to watch both movies within a week during that time. This happened to be a series of sequels to the earlier Hong Kong box office successes - Ip Man I released in 2008 and Ip Man II in 2010. Each of these martial art exponents, followed by their trademark Wing Chun, struck me deeply as emotionally invincible men. The lead protagonist in Ip Man I and Ip Man II, Grandmaster Ip Man, not only defeated his opponents in terms of martial arts techniques but also illustrated emotional resilience in his mind after each fight. On the other hand, Grandmaster Ip Man's young protege in the preceding prequel, The Legend is Born, was meek and unassuming. However, this young man's emotional resilience culminated in him rising victoriously out of his self-imposed mental prison, which was more important.

2.3. Cultivating Emotional Resilience: The Essence of Achieving Freedom

2.4. Practicing Mindfulness

Academics have begun studying emotional intelligence for increased issue resolution and momentum in the reduction of workplace issues. Research revealed that these results weren't simply a function of more emotionally intelligent individuals being popular and broadly well-liked; members of the high emotional intelligence team were not only better at exhibiting support, perspective taking, and encouragement, they also modeled conflict management strategies more successfully. For organizations seeking to inspire happier, more productive employees, developing emotional intelligence is the first step towards that goal. Just like learning to appreciate the diversity of perspectives and experiences within our organizations ultimately yields better problem-solving and innovation, understanding and prioritizing our social interactions in the workplace may end in our staff building camaraderie, trust, and overall job satisfaction.

If you're familiar with the concept of emotional intelligence (EQ), you have probably heard of the importance of practicing mindfulness. At first glance, these ideas – the psychological construct predicting our capacity to navigate the social world, and the spiritual practice encouraging attention to the present – may seem somewhat unrelated. Practice in areas such as meditation, however, has shown tangible gains in domains associated with emotional intelligence, such as self-regulation. In fact, office environments implementing regular mindfulness-based interventions report both lower employee stress and higher cognitive flexibility, two heavily woven factors in the construct of emotional intelligence. Whether through the practice of meditation itself or other attention training exercises, cultivating mindfulness appears foundational to developing a greater understanding of oneself and others.

CHAPTER 3

Building Empathy and Social Skills

Autonomy is most likely to benefit from the autonomy of this all-embracing, balancing kind of empathy. However perfect your reasoning, however timely your responses, however exquisitely their words may seem to soar beyond the constraints of linguistic communication and slip into your heart, if you fail to respond to the person you are counseling, you are not thereby providing counsel. Empathy does not manifest itself only in our words to show that we understand; it shows in our actions. It demonstrates a real concern for the well-being because it opens them up to speak and to stand up and keeps them open so they can access what is deeply significant. Empathy follows no growth model, because the need behind the empathy of the growing moment and the unique depths of the parties it connects are always of the most legitimate and vital potential. Made to cultivate life-giving relationships that foster life-enriching contribution, the nonviolent communication teaches us how to alter a selfish compass to recognize the basic needs of all people.

To develop the social and emotional skills that channel autonomy and empathy in service of a life of purpose, there may be no one better to consult than psychologist Marshall B. Rosenberg, who in 1984 founded the Center for Nonviolent Communication and is the author of the seminal book, Nonviolent Communication: A Language of Life. Expressing our needs and feelings, Rosenberg says, is crucial for fostering life-enriching relationships, and understanding others' needs and feelings is essential to meeting those needs and enriching our own lives in the process. Experiencing empathy for yourself - just like experiencing anger, fear, assurance, and appreciation, all of which are vital components of this process - engages empathy in others. In the empathy and social skills that spring to life when you steadfastly develop autonomy - the independence to think and act on your own but always in service of helping others do the same - and put autonomy to the cause of aiding others.

3.1. Empathetic Listening

A restatement involves repeating what the person has said as accurately as possible. It is not in response to the feelings of the listener or quick advice. Instead, a restatement is a simple repetition of the content of the individual's message. Additionally, a clarification statement is where you help the speaker translate and clarify what they have just said. You can do this simply by saying, "That felt disrespectful," which helps the speaker roughly identify their emotions and beliefs. Lastly, perception checking involves letting the individual know what your perceptions are. In talking to them, you want to share your perception, your message of them at that moment in your reaction. The understanding of the speaker is not important. What counts is giving and receiving a message. It is a key to boosting the listener's EQ.

Empathetic listening is an essential skill for boosting another's emotional clarity. By actively acknowledging another person's feelings and thoughts, you guide them to a sense of understanding, which can help defuse tension. You acknowledge their emotions by being an empathetic listener who accurately perceives their feelings and perspectives and communicates that understanding to them. You do not have to agree with the person's feelings or responses to empathize, as the object is to acknowledge the individual's emotional load. Remember, the words need to communicate their feelings to you.

3.2. Effective Communication

By learning to be more excellent at paying attention to and articulating what is truly going on, you become superb at understanding and communicating on. There are two significant types of communication: committed and passive. Passive behaviour is where you fail to communicate, or where you thoughtlessly use lazily use unoriginal answers. The passive path is the easy path, because it is worldwide and everyone can go that route. The other path is where you focus on the conversation and prepare to be engaged. You genuinely care about your staff, and you work hard to communicate with them. Of the two paths, the passive route is the easier and more commonly used. It is unfortunate that the passive route is used in 90% of conversations because it perpetuates a cycle of bland and ignorant responses.

We communicate with each other in many ways. These include written words in reports and emails, and our speech, but also our facial expressions, our gestures, and our tone. Over 60% of our communication to others is by our body language, not by the words themselves. As such, ensuring that we can work powerfully with others is crucial in any industry today. It is a cop-out to say that you cannot communicate as well as you would like to, because learning excellent communication skills is much easier when you work at it.

3.3. Conflict Resolution

When I used to work for a luxury resort, I had a boss that would lose her temper when things would go "wrong" during the shift. If we had a bad day due to weather or lack of business, she would be stressed to the max by the end of it, and would lash at all of us, regardless if it was our fault or not. She also would rarely listen to what we have to say, and if she did she would make a big deal out of it. As a result, none of us were motivated and we did not have respect for her as a leader. After years of being there, I realized the importance of putting yourself in someone else's shoes, and how everything could have been avoided. In case of an unresolved issues, you know when you have the option to keep something to yourself or to sit down and talk about it. Especially if it is bothering you. If you decide to keep it to yourself, the problem will not go away—we tend to stress over it, even if we don't want to, and that will end up making us emotional and perhaps make the situation worse than it is.

But we define EQ as understanding, using, managing and influencing emotions. That is, 1. knowing what you're feeling and why you are feeling it. 2. being able to select which emotions you focus on—and which you let pass. 3. managing your emotions and 4. being able to influence and motivate yourself and others. In order to succeed in fixing an issue, you have to understand why things are the way they are, and being able to talk to team members, and understand their concerns, fears, and insecurities. It is important to have real communication to be able to understand the emotional reactions of the people involved without becoming upset yourself.

When emotional intelligence first appeared to the masses, it served as the missing link in a peculiar finding: people with average IQs outperform those with the highest IQs 70% of the time. This anomaly threw a massive wrench into what many people had always assumed was the sole source of success—IQ. Decades of research now point to emotional intelligence as being the critical sine qua non of leadership. That's why we've found that people often define high EQ as the quality of making emotional competencies consistent with their actions.

3.4. Collaboration and Teamwork

Making decisions often involves a team-oriented approach. Oftentimes, individuals from various business departments are brought together and given the task of coming up with a solution to a problem. Interaction between contributors is important; however, when an individual is low in their emotional intelligence, the level of collaboration and teamwork suffers, causing an organization to incur costs and decreases in productivity. Antonakis and Dietz suggested that when leaders displayed the EI skills of optimism, humor, enthusiasm, and inspiration, performance was increased. CO photographs receive high performance ratings having a supportive work environment. Their leadership skills abilities resulted in a positive organizational culture evident in the following employee behaviors: a conducive work environment, increased productivity, motivation to excel, and hard work. A study by Gong, Sam, and Baer showed that emotional intelligence is a key predictor for business leaders to influence, lead change, and collaborate, thus ensuring that management works towards a shared organizational goal.

Mayer and Salovey described a specific form of emotional intelligence referred to as strategic emotion control. It involves the ability to read others more effectively and to interact with others on a more personal level. Better relationships with others are apparent through more effective communication and better collaboration skills. Job duties for an HR professional may include working with diverse individuals in a company. Bondarouk and Ruël found that emotional intelligence was a significant predictor for professionals who work in the HR department to succeed. It is evident that when HR professionals have enhanced their EI through EI training, their work relationship with peers or staff, teamwork, and leadership skills are also enhanced. Kawachat suggested a training program for HR professionals to develop their emotional intelligence to enhance their teamwork and leadership skills and to improve their relationships with clients. Hence, developing their own EI helps them to become generalists and to have the strategic business-driven capability necessary to contribute to long-term business goals of an organization.

CHAPTER 4

Applying Emotional Intelligence in Various Areas

II.1 INTRODUCTION Emotional expressions - both "real" and "felt" - have become increasingly important in a service environment. In an especially competitive market, Emotional Intelligence (EI), or how emotions are felt and contemplated, is considered one of the important points for sales and customer services performance. Previous research has shown that Emotional Intelligence is a key factor in organizational performance. Furthermore, EI has been recently investigated in relation to organizational outcomes, which include the EI of its individuals. In the sales and marketing area, EI plays an important role in winning business and increasing profitability.

The contribution of this study enhances sales and customer services performance by responsible human resources. Because a change in a salesman's emotion may change sales results, managers and salespeople will have a better understanding of emotional intelligence as a new tool to use in the process of sales force effectiveness.

In sales and customer services, nowadays, with more focus on customer relationships and employees' attitude towards customer services, organizations require a higher level of EI in both sales and customer services. Salespeople with high levels of EI are able to effectively motivate and bring progress to their interactions with customers. Because they better understand clients' psychological and emotional needs, salespeople with high EI can enhance the quality of their service to the customer. There is a relationship between high EI of sellers and a high degree of customer satisfaction and loyalty. Our findings also support previous research on customer services, showing that a high level of EI in CSRs can increase customer satisfaction. Managerial implications and limitations of this research are discussed. Keywords: The article aims to discover the effects of Emotional Intelligence on two aspects affecting organizational performance: sales and customer services. The research results revealed that the higher the Emotional Intelligence degree, the higher the sales level and greater customer satisfaction. There was also a significant relationship between sales and customer satisfaction, and between EI and customer satisfaction.

4.1. Emotional Intelligence in Leadership

When that self-discipline is in place and you are practicing good character, there is something magnetic about you that inspires other people to good actions. Character is infectious; the more of it you have, the more of those traits you'll see in others. Still, the big thing to realize about emotional intelligence is that it affects others. I am always reminded about a friend of mine that had a sign up in his office that said "Others". He said, "I brought it in the office to remind myself that in my job there is nothing more important than my relationships with other people". If you look at any book on emotional intelligence, it states that there are many ingredients to emotional intelligence. One of the best articles on the subject was written by Daniel Goleman called "What Makes a Leader" in the Harvard Business Review. When Goleman's article first appeared, it was the most requested reprint in the history of the fifteen-year-old HBR.

The ability to control yourself is the most important determinant of how good a leader you become. Leadership starts from within. Ask yourself, "Who am I trying to lead? My answer would be life. And I can't do it very well at all until I realize that I first have to lead myself. I am the leader of me." I like to define leadership as the ability to make the tough choices in life and the willingness to do the right thing no matter how hard it is. It's not always easy and for most of us, self-discipline and emotional intelligence are things that we don't see much of in the world today. One of the things that is interesting about great leaders is that they know that self-discipline is the root of good character and is the foundation for emotional intelligence.

4.2. Emotional Intelligence in the Workplace

- In a 2011 survey of more than 2600 hiring managers and HR professionals, 71% said they value emotional intelligence over IQ. The study also found that workers with high emotional intelligence tended to earn more than those with lower levels. 75% of survey respondents said they would be more likely to promote a worker with high emotional intelligence over one with a high IQ. This correlation has been confirmed in a comprehensive analysis conducted by Virginia Commonwealth University, which showed that every point increase in overall EQ results in a $1300 annual increase in salary. Furthermore, the higher a worker's rank in an organization, the more overall EQ contributes to his or her salary. Workers at the highest rank, or "most desirable" level of leadership, earned an average of $29,000 more annually, suggesting that EQ is even more valuable—and more financially rewarded—when there is a greater degree of employee interaction required to perform a job. And yes, you read that correctly. There was a minimum IQ threshold of about 124 points, but a person with an average IQ (about 100 points) and high emotional intelligence pathways better than one with high IQ but average emotional intelligence.

Consider the following research findings from Travis Bradberry and Jean Greaves in Emotional Intelligence 2.0:

What makes a great employee? Many people answer this question by saying, "Someone who works hard." While it may be true that hard work is a necessary component of success, it is also possible to work hard and still be a subpar employee. Instead, the best employees are ones who can understand others, manage their own emotions, and use their understanding to communicate and collaborate effectively. In other words, the best employees are those who have high emotional intelligence (EQ). And if you're responsible for any hiring, developing, or coaching of employees, emotional intelligence is absolutely critical to success. Take it from me. My consulting practice focuses on solving high levels of interpersonal workplace conflict, disengagement, and lack of productivity, and emotional intelligence is always a factor.

4.3. Emotional Intelligence in Relationships

But from the very moment we 'move in', resistance builds and invariably a pile of negative evidence starts growing. More so when we subject ourselves to constant criticism. Every time one makes a mistake in the new job, there would be a sense of questioning, "Was taking up this wrong?" Have reliable relationships get eroded. The same thing happens at home or even with friends. Of course, the specific dynamics are a little different, but the underlying relationships are strongly disrupted by conflicts. Effectively handling situations, battling those lies, and showing a high degree of emotional maturity - making sure that the "German Shepherd is fed" is of paramount importance to enter sound, mature long-term relationships.

Emotional intelligence in relationships - Relationship management is the heart of EQ - that's what we have been discussing so far. Managing relationships isn't easy. People aren't rational, robots. They are emotional, irrational, and behave in a highly unpredictable manner. At the onset of every new relationship (be it at home, in the office, or with friends), all we see is 'positive evidence'. That's a normal thing to happen. When we meet people for the first time, start a job for the first time, or get into a new situation for the first time, people welcome us with open arms. There is simply no reason for things to go wrong. It's next to impossible to predict what one may go through at a later point in time.

Milton Keynes UK
Ingram Content Group UK Ltd.
UKHW030908271124
451618UK00011B/334